GORILLAS
AND THEIR BABIES

MARIANNE JOHNSTON

The Rosen Publishing Group's
PowerKids Press™
New York

Special thanks to Diane Shapiro of the Bronx Zoo for making this project possible.

Published in 1999 by The Rosen Publishing Group, Inc.
29 East 21st Street, New York, NY 10010

First Edition

Book design : Resa Listort

Photo Credits: All photos © Wildlife Conservation Society.

Johnston, Marianne.
     Gorillas and their babies / by Marianne Johnston.
         p.   cm. — (A zoo life book)
   Includes index.
   Summary: Describes the characteristics of gorillas and how mother gorillas living in zoos are taught to care for their babies.
   ISBN 0-8239-5313-0
   1. Gorilla—Juvenile literature. 2. Gorilla—Infancy—Juvenile literature. 3. Zoo animals—Juvenile literature.
[1. Gorilla. 2. Animals—Infancy. 3. Zoo animals.] I. Title. II. Series: Johnston, Marianne. Zoo life book.
   QL737.P96C688 1998
   599.884—DC21
                                                     98-23986
                                                     CIP
                                                     AC

Manufactured in the United States of America

CONTENTS

THE GORILLA

Watching a baby gorilla tumbling and playing at a zoo is a lot like watching a human baby play. That's because the gentle gorilla is a close **relative** (REH-luh-tiv) of humans.

There are three kinds of gorillas. They are all found in Africa. The mountain gorilla lives in the mountains of central Africa. There are also two kinds of **lowland** (LOH-land) gorillas. These gorillas live in the **rain forests** (RAYN FOR-ists) along the western coast of central Africa.

More than 350 lowland gorillas live in zoos all around North America. Zoos play a big part in saving these **endangered** (en-DAYN-jerd) animals.

ORDER:
PRIMATES
FAMILY:
PONGIDAE
GENUS & SPECIES:
GORILLA GORILLA

◀ Zoos provide places for young gorillas to live and grow safely.

WHAT ARE GORILLAS LIKE?

Gorillas are the largest **primates** (PRY-mayts). Primates are a group of animals that includes monkeys, gorillas, and humans. Male gorillas can weigh over 450 pounds. Female gorillas weigh about 200 pounds. Gorillas can live to be 50 years old.

Like humans, gorillas are very **social** (SOH-shul). They take care of one another and spend lots of time with their families. In the wild, gorillas spend up to half their day finding and eating different kinds of fruit and plants. Gorillas mostly stay on the ground, moving around from place to place. Each night, they build a new nest to sleep in.

Older gorillas watch the young gorillas at play, just like someone looks out for you. ▶

WHAT DOES A ZOO DO?

At a zoo, you can see many different kinds of animals that you would usually have to travel thousands of miles to see in the wild. But zoos do a lot more than allow people to look at wildlife. Zoos also save endangered animals.

Gorillas are in great danger in their African homeland. There, humans are destroying gorillas' **habitats** (HA-bih-tats) to clear land for farming.

Zoos around the world provide gorillas with safe homes. Zoos also give gorilla families a place where they can have more babies. Zoos are trying to save the gorilla from **extinction** (ek-STINKT-shun).

◀ Animals at a zoo are kept in areas that are built to look like their natural homes.

9

A GORILLA FAMILY

There are usually between ten and twenty gorillas in a gorilla family. As a male grows up, a large, silvery patch of fur appears across his back. This grown-up male is called a silverback. The silverback gorilla leads and protects an entire gorilla family. Young males, several females, and their babies make up the rest of the family.

The silverback gorilla will often play with the young gorillas. He even lets the baby gorillas climb on him!

Gorillas aren't fully grown until they are about ten years old.

In the wild, when males turn ten, they move on to start their own families. ▶

LEARNING TO BE A MOTHER

Female gorillas learn how to be good mothers by watching mother gorillas raise their babies. A young female will also help take care of her younger brothers and sisters. This is the way she learns how to hold them and play with them. When she has her own babies, she will be ready to be a good mother.

Life in a zoo is different from life in the wild. Female gorillas that are raised in zoos have never learned how to care for baby gorillas. When they have their own babies, these gorillas might not know how to take care of them. Humans will then help the mother gorilla to **raise** (RAYZ) her new baby.

◀ Young gorillas like to spend time playing with the rest of the family.

TEACHING GORILLAS TO BE GOOD MOTHERS

Because they haven't been taught how to raise a baby, female gorillas in zoos may ignore their babies. Without a mother's attention and milk, a baby would die. This is when humans will take over.

If a female that was raised in a zoo is **pregnant** (PREG-nunt), zookeepers let the gorilla practice caring for a baby with a doll. They teach the gorilla how to hold the doll and cuddle with it. When the gorilla gives birth, the zookeepers hope she will have learned enough to care for her baby just as she cared for the doll. Other females in that gorilla family are able to learn how to care for their babies by watching the new gorilla mother.

Like human babies, gorilla babies need lots of help and attention. ▶

THE FIRST FEW MONTHS

When a baby gorilla is born, it is helpless, just like a human baby. During the first month of its life, a baby gorilla must be held by her mother. The baby is not yet strong enough to hold on to her mom by herself. Like all **mammals** (MA-mulz), a baby gorilla drinks her mother's milk. This is the only food the baby gorilla eats for the first few months.

As she gets older and stronger, the baby will start to eat solid foods, such as berries and leaves. Soon the baby gorilla is strong enough to hold on to its mother and ride around on her back. At about three months, the baby begins to crawl.

◀ A young gorilla can get a piggyback ride if she is too tired to crawl.

RAISED BY HUMANS

If a mother gorilla cannot take care of her own baby, then the baby must be raised by humans. These baby gorillas are raised in a zoo **nursery** (NER-ser-ee). Some nurseries have cribs where the baby gorillas can sleep, just like human babies do. Baby gorillas wear diapers too. The zookeeper may wear a thick, furry blanket over his chest when he feeds the baby gorilla from a bottle. To the baby, this blanket feels like a mother gorilla's chest.

Some zoos have playgrounds with jungle gyms, balls, and toys for the young gorillas to play with. They play with these things just like human kids do!

It is a very exciting time at a zoo when a baby gorilla is born. ▶

WHEN GORILLAS ADOPT

When a gorilla baby that has been raised by humans turns two, zookeepers try to bring her into a gorilla family. This takes some time, but gorillas usually don't mind **adopting** (uh-DOP-ting) a young gorilla. In fact, gorillas in the wild adopt **orphaned** (OR-fund) babies too.

First the zookeepers will introduce a baby gorilla to just one member of the gorilla family, usually a female. They hope the female will take care of the young gorilla. Once they are sure the female will protect the young gorilla, the two are brought together into the gorilla family.

◀ Being part of a family helps young gorillas learn important skills, such as how to find food.

THE GORILLA'S FUTURE

There are only about 50,000 lowland gorillas left in the wild. Only a few hundred mountain gorillas remain in the mountains of Africa. Laws have been passed to protect gorillas. But **poachers** (POH-churz) continue to kill them. Poachers kill mother gorillas to get their babies. When a baby gorilla's mother is hurt, the baby stays by its mother. This makes it easy for poachers to take the babies and sell them to zoos. Most zoos will not accept "orphaned" baby gorillas. Zookeepers hope that this will help stop poachers. Zoos around the world are working together to save gorillas and protect their future.

WEB SITE

You can learn more about gorillas at this Web site: http://www.gorilla-haven.org/

GLOSSARY

adopt (uh-DOPT) When an older animal raises a baby animal that has lost its own parents.

endangered (en-DAYN-jerd) When something is in danger of no longer existing.

extinct (ek-STINKT) To no longer exist.

habitat (HA-bih-tat) The surroundings where an animal lives.

lowland (LOH-land) A section of land that is lower and flatter than the land around it.

mammal (MA-mul) An animal that is warm-blooded, breathes oxygen, and gives birth to live young.

nursery (NER-ser-ee) A special place where baby gorillas are born, cared for, and raised.

orphan (OR-fun) When a young animal loses its mother.

poacher (POH-chur) A person who illegally kills animals that are protected by the law.

pregnant (PREG-nunt) When a female has a baby or babies growing inside her.

primate (PRY-mayt) The group of animals that includes monkeys, gorillas, and humans.

rain forest (RAYN FOR-ist) A very wet area that has many kinds of plants, trees, and animals.

raise (RAYZ) To bring up a baby.

relative (REH-luh-tiv) Something that comes from the same ancestors as you.

social (SOH-shul) Living and breeding in organized communities.

INDEX